OWLS IN OUR YARD!

OWLS IN OUR YARD!

The Story of Alfie

CARL SAFINA

Norton Young Readers

An Imprint of W. W. Norton & Company
Independent Publishers Since 1923

TO ALL WHO CARE FOR THE WILD ONES.

Copyright © 2024 by Carl Safina
Photos on pages 9, 16, and 17 courtesy of Patricia M. Paladines
Illustrations copyright © Tatsuro Kiuchi

All rights reserved
Printed in China
First Edition

For information about permission to reproduce selections from this book,
write to Permissions, W. W. Norton & Company, Inc., 500 Fifth Avenue, New York, NY 10110

For information about special discounts for bulk purchases, please contact
W. W. Norton Special Sales at specialsales@wwnorton.com or 800-233-4830

Manufacturing by RRD Asia
Book design by Hana Anouk Nakamura
Production manager: Delaney Adams

ISBN 978-1-324-05319-4

W. W. Norton & Company, Inc., 500 Fifth Avenue, New York, N.Y. 10110
www.wwnorton.com

W. W. Norton & Company Ltd., 15 Carlisle Street, London W1D 3BS

1 2 3 4 5 6 7 8 9 0

In the photo it looked like a wet washcloth. The text message explained that this creature was found on the ground. Some kind of baby bird. Barely alive. No nest in sight.

This baby's fluff was full of dirt. And something worse: blowfly eggs. If they hatched, the fly larvae—called maggots—would eat the poor little bird alive!

I knew what to do. I'd had permits to take care of unlucky wildlife, and I'd helped injured birds before.

Washed, dabbed dry, and warmed by the wildlife rehabilitator who'd texted me, the chick still looked so messed up that it wasn't obvious what kind of bird this was. But I realized that this little one was an owl. Small enough to fit into my palm—so that meant this was a baby eastern screech owl.

They nest in dark holes in trees. Somehow, this owlet had been dragged and dropped. Perhaps by a raiding crow? Was this messy nestling the only survivor? The luckiest one of a very unlucky brood? No way to know. But some good luck had arrived.

And so this babe got saved, and began to grow and thrive.

🐦 🐦 🐦

Our dogs, Chula, Jude, and Cady, were friendly with small birds. They had grown up around our little flock of free-roving chickens.

Alfie needed a steady source of good food. Owls are hunters. Online, I found a source of frozen mice and sent for some.

Alfie, a few days after she was rescued.

The home crew: Jude, Chula, Patricia, Cady.

Alfie in her first juvenile feathers.

When a wild baby bird grows big enough to fly, they leave their nest. Parent owls care for and feed their young ones for several weeks afterward. During that time, young ones practice to be expert fliers while learning how to catch food. Eventually, like young people, they move away from their parents and start their own lives.

Our plan was: let Alfie decide when she was ready to fly away. Meanwhile, we'd keep her safe and well (and protect her at night in our mudroom). To help Alfie develop an active mind and a strong body, we often let her join us while we were outside doing things like gardening.

But soon we realized that Alfie had a problem. Her body and head feathers had grown out nicely. And the longest wing feathers were growing beautifully. But the other wing feathers necessary for flight were not coming in at all. Most of each wing was bare. Maybe she would *never* fly.

Alfie joins our daughter, Alex, me, and doggies after a morning's clam-digging. At the time, we worried that Alfie might never fly.

In early autumn, when she was three months old, Alfie molted all her feathers. The fluffy pajamas of her baby days dropped out. Little by little, she grew a sleek new set of adult feathers. Her wing feathers grew beautifully—all of them! Now her wings were perfect. And she could fly!

Alfie was gorgeous. Her long new wing feathers had waves of light and dark banding. Black "eyeliner" made her large eyes utterly striking. The feathers that help funnel sound into special ear openings gave her a typical owl face. Cream-colored feathers created eyebrows like little clouds. Feathered tufts shaped like cats' ears poked above the round outline of her head. Below her throat, a line traveled down to her toes like a drip of ice cream.

Most of her head, back, wings, and tail were brick-red. But dark chocolate streaks gave her camouflage. If feeling threatened, she could stretch up like an elongated branch, squinting to make her eyes disappear, and erecting those head-feathers like little sticks. Then she would look like tree bark.

With two toes facing front and two facing backward, an owl has four evenly spaced claws, called talons, on each foot. They are like curved needles for grabbing small animals such as mice and bugs.

Alfie, gorgeous and perfect in new adult feathers.

Alfie could swivel her head in famous owlish fashion—about three-quarters of the way around. Try doing that! Owls have about fourteen neck bones, giving them a wide range of motion. (Mammals—humans, even giraffes—have seven.) Blood vessels and spinal cord nerves run through the bones in roomy canals; that way, they don't get pinched when the owl swivels their head. Pretty cool.

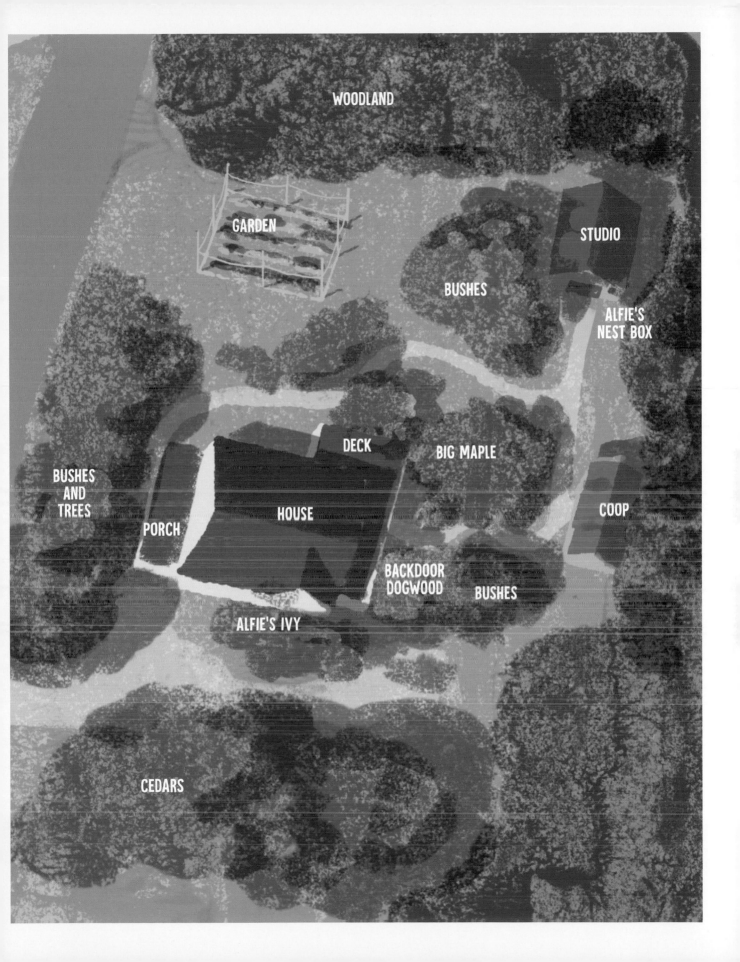

Now Alfie had all her feathers and could fly. But all during summer when she could not fly, she had not been able to learn how to hunt. By late October, nights got chilly. The field crickets' calls were slowing. Soon they would be gone. Letting Alfie wander off into a world with temperatures getting too cool for crickets, moths, and other insects that she might eat seemed like a big risk. If she flew away now, she might starve.

So we made a decision. I prepared the outdoor portion of our chicken coop for her. We continued feeding her. And there, safe from the possibility of starvation, she spent the winter. She was comfortable. But I was not. An owl who is not out doing owly things is just a bird in a cage. That's not the life I wanted for her.

Alfie was comfortable in the coop, but this wasn't the life she was born to live.

When summer returned, I started letting Alfie fly from the coop to me for food. I'd open the door and walk a few steps away, then hold up her favorite defrosted mouse or piece of fresh fish. It was practice for a wider freedom. It was the right thing to do.

One day, I opened the door, walked out about ten steps, turned, and offered Alfie a morning meal. She fluttered out and landed on my arm. But she did not take the food.

Instead, her big eyes scanned the wider world, scanned the trees, scanned the sky. Taking it all in.

She suddenly flew up into a maple tree. Then she came down low enough for me to give her some food and pick her up and put her in the coop. This time I left the door open.

The next morning, food I'd left was still there. I called. And called. No answer, no Alfie.

My fear had been that Alfie would wander off and starve. Now, that was a real possibility.

In the coop everything had been safe. But she could never live the life she was born to live. I knew Alfie had made the best choice. Freedom, however, was dangerous. Choosing freedom might hurt. Might get her killed. I worried greatly.

Getting Alfie ready for her free-flying life: she flies from the coop to take a meal from my hand.

A few days after Alfie's disappearance, I had to disappear for a few days myself on a trip. Food that my wife, Patricia, left out each night remained untouched each morning. The week passed with no sign of Alfie.

🐿 🐿 🐿

The night before I was scheduled to head home, a ding from my cell phone woke me. A text from Patricia read, "Guess who's back!"

Patricia was sitting outside after dark when Alfie showed up. Alfie followed Patricia to the coop. Alfie went in. Patricia gave her food.

Alfie's week-long disappearance had made me worry a lot. But she *hadn't* starved. So we continued to leave the door open, even though autumn was again approaching.

Alfie was finally making her own choices. She had become a free-living owl, yet she chose to keep the connection with us. We saw her nightly. She often came close enough for a little head scratching and took treats. And she began snoozing through the daylight hours in the protection of thick ivy growing on a huge old maple tree outside our bedroom window.

Alfie's world was enlarging. But our world was about to get smaller.

I get an owly kiss.

Alfie usually spent daylight in the ivy outside our bedroom window.

Alfie in the backdoor dogwood.

Around New Year's, we read newspaper reports about people getting sick with a new illness. Soon that new illness got a name: coronavirus disease—Co-Vi-D for short. Soon Covid found many countries. Too soon, people were getting sick where we lived.

And suddenly the life we knew—of visiting, going out, going into classrooms, going to work, of family holidays, our ways of being in the world—went away. Everyone was upset and worried.

How very strange that upset seemed when we saw how Alfie was so at home in the world, so comfortable being herself in her own nature. Alfie was showing us a way of living that was slower, calmer. Alfie's magic was perfectly timed to help us, when we needed to find a way to feel that things were OK.

Plus-One, left. On the right, a very relaxed Alfie.

One morning at the end of the first week of March, Patricia peered up into the deep shade of Alfie's ivy. Looking down at her with head-feather tufts straight up, eyes squinted nearly closed, and body stretched like a branch, was a screech owl.

"That's not—*Alfie*," she thought. Patricia circled the tree and saw a second owl, fluffed and relaxed as usual. Alfie. Patricia called to me. "Alfie has a buddy."

That evening, Alfie did not return our calls. That night, Alfie showed no interest in food. She was in owl love.

Alfie was helping us see a larger circle of life that we all shared. Spring was in the air.

Flocks of red-winged blackbirds, grackles, and robins flowed northward. Going nowhere myself, I watched a living world very much on the move.

Alfie and her buddy—we named him Plus-One—usually spent the day roosting together. If they did not, they would meet at sunset. Alfie sometimes called, "*Ooh. Ooh. Ooh.*" It meant, "I'm here, where are you?"

From the woods, Plus-One answered. Usually he'd go and catch something, like a moth, and feed it to her.

Alfie, right, accepts a moth from Plus-One.

Alfie looks at Patricia from her nest box while Patricia looks for Plus-One.

Because Alfie now had a mate and they both liked our backyard, I put up a nesting house specially designed for screech owls. Alfie and Plus-One checked some holes in big old trees, but decided they liked the nest box best. I saw them both go in and out.

Eventually I realized that Alfie, alone, was in the box all day. At sundown she would come out for just a few minutes, fly to the bird bath and take a drink, and go right back to the nest box. Something was going on in there.

Alfie visited the bird bath as the sun was setting.

Alfie's first eggs!

One night I waited for her to come out, then quickly put up a
ladder, climbed to the nest box, stuck my phone into the entrance,
and took several photos. I scrambled down and removed the ladder
quickly so everything would look normal when Alfie came back.
And then I checked the photos. And sure enough, Alfie was caring
for—eggs! How great!

In the middle of May, when I calculated that Alfie's eggs were
due to hatch, I did the same thing. Waited. Put up the ladder. Got
several photos. Scrambled down before she came back.

I was *delighted* by what the photos revealed. Alfie now had three
little owlets to protect and feed. And were they ever tiny! *All three*
newly hatched owls together were no bigger than one little wild white-
footed mouse that their father, Plus-One, had delivered to the nest.

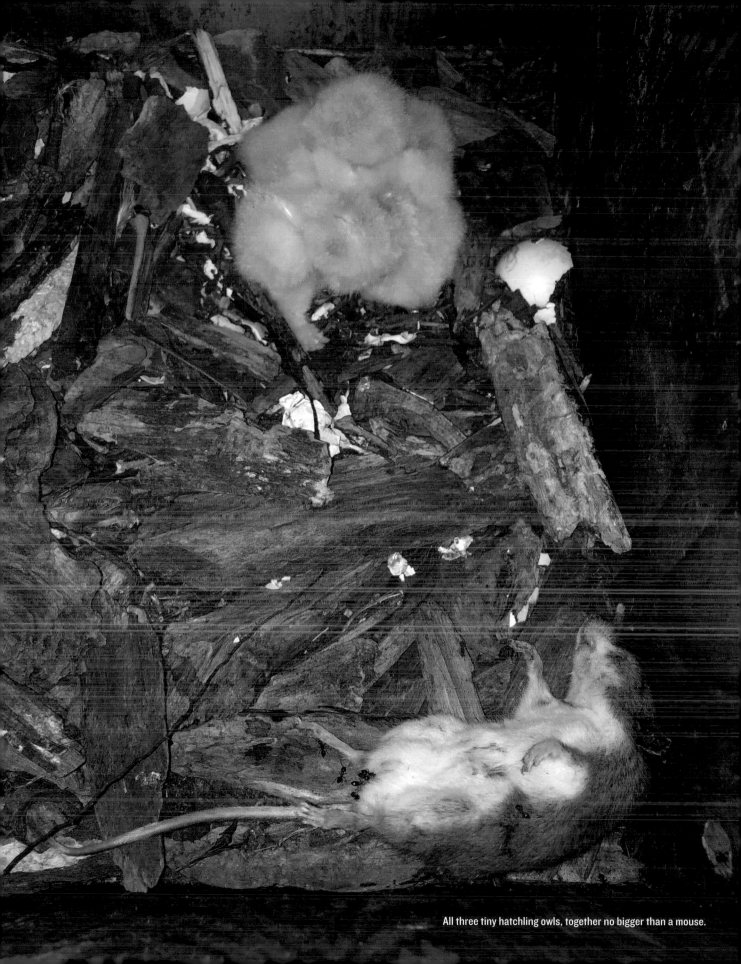
All three tiny hatchling owls, together no bigger than a mouse.

Babies getting bigger.

During the second week of June, the young ones were getting big. The little nest box was getting crowded. From time to time owlets of slightly differing sizes peeked out. Bobbing and waving their heads, they were learning how to bring the world into focus.

One evening, one of Alfie's three owlets came out and stood on the little platform right outside the nest-box entrance. A sibling knocked that one off balance, causing them to hang on upside down. It was a ridiculous moment. But that little one was strong, and soon got themself right side up.

One baby almost lost their grip
but hung on—and got back up.

After dark, something hit the metal awning over the door below the nest box.

Cady showed up and started barking very excitedly. Now I heard bill-clacking from the ground.

I went for a flashlight.

I was suddenly looking down at a someone who looked like cotton candy with big eyes staring up at me.

Cady kept her eyes on the owlet while half her body wagged her excitement.

I called Patricia. Chula and Jude came too, hurrying along. The little owl must have been surprised that the world outside the nest box was so full of people and dogs!

Alfie was nearby, calling.

We kept trying to put the little owlet up in a tree. The owlet kept slipping, hanging upside down, or falling to the ground. But the ground could be dangerous. Cats roam our neighborhood, and raccoons, and even an occasional fox.

All three owlets, staring out at the big world they'd soon join.

So we continued putting the owl up into the safety of branches. We tried a tree. We tried a bush. But the little one kept coming down.

On and on it went like this, up and down, down and up, for a while. Finally, the youngster stayed up in a tree.

Alfie acted anxious. She was a new mom who had never before seen a babe out of the nest. She repeatedly landed right next to her newly fledged young one.

Alfie's other two owlets crowded the nest entrance, staring out at the world they would soon be part of. They seemed amazed by it all.

Alfie and a youngster snuggling at the nest.

Early the next morning two blue jays discovered the young one in the tree. The jays were not happy. Owls can be a danger to blue jay nestlings. Striking hard with their bills, the jays tried to knock the young owl to the ground.

Alfie launched an attack to defend her baby. The jays withdrew to a nearby branch and seemed to think about what to do next. They decided to leave—at least for a little while.

🦉 🦉 🦉

On the ground, looking up at the home they'd just left.

That evening at sunset, Alfie's other two young owlets left the
nest. They looked like little snowmen, their fluffy down light gray,
their heads round as a generous scoop of ice cream.

The young ones could not fly well. When they tried, they usually
missed the branch they were aiming for. They would end up on the
ground. But amazingly, they could walk straight up the trunks of
trees!

After the sun went down, one lone firefly—the very first of the
year—glowed on and off through the shadows of night. The fledged
trio of young owls perched in trees at the edge of the woods.

They got all of Alfie's attention.

And ours.

Alfie abruptly went back into the nest box, quickly turned around
in there, and looked out, calling softly. Maybe she needed to be sure
that it was now empty and no one was left behind.

The next morning, all three owlets (and Alfie) were alive and well, a great start to a beautiful day.

But then jays and robins found the owls. And right away, things got very rough.

In fast-streaking attacks they made sharp, hard contact, smacking one of the youngsters to the ground.

After about five minutes on the ground, this chick started climbing up the trunk. Partway up, the owlet again got knocked to the ground.

Alfie shot out of her nest box and rushed the jay.

The jay turned—to threaten Alfie.

And now two jays slammed a second owlet.

Hanging upside down, the youngster received several added smacks, got knocked loose, and fell like an apple, hitting the ground hard.

A blue jay knocked a youngster out of the tree. But the young owls could *walk* up tree trunks!

Alfie seemed startled by the severity of the attacks. She was in some danger too. This was no game. Those beaks were sharp and the jays and robins did *not* want owls out and about in their own nesting territory near their own helpless jay and robin nestlings. A robin streaked in and tore a feather from Alfie's head.

The young one on the ground began another climb. And *again* got knocked out of the tree—and fell to the ground.

Wow. The first few hours in the big world were harsh!

🐿 🐿 🐿

Shortly after that, all the owls got into a dense bush. They huddled up. Alfie was guarding. When attackers approached, she threatened. When attackers withdrew, everyone relaxed.

Tenderness. Alfie preened one of her babies, who then preened her. Their bills gently nibbled around the head, eyes, bill, and neck.

Two blue jays arrived, then left.

The young owls were out in the world and would never return to the nest box. But they had each other.

After that morning, there were no more attacks from jays and robins. The young ones got stronger and life got easier. We named the group of youngsters "The Hoo."

Alfie and Plus-One continued protecting, caring for, and feeding The Hoo for a few weeks. At sundown, the youngsters often followed their parents around our backyard and into our neighbors' yards. Plus-One, a very skillful hunter, would deliver food, and The Hoo were always well fed.

Eventually all young beings must leave their parents and create their own lives.

And in midsummer, that's what happened. The young ones started going farther. One morning, they were gone. It was the best possible ending to a story that continues.

The Hoo.

Plus-One bringing
a chipmunk to his
young ones.

Alfie remained our magical presence of the nighttime backyard. A year later, she was sitting on new eggs. She was in the same nest box on the outer wall of my writing room, just outside my window.

I walked outside. She heard my footsteps and she called to me.

I replied, "Hello, Alfie."

It wasn't the end of her story. It was another new beginning.

At this writing, Alfie has raised three broods and put ten new screech owls out into the world. We see her frequently. She continues to add a touch of magic to our lives. There are always "owls in our yard!"

Alfie came a long way from having been found near death as a baby to becoming a successful mother to her own young ones.

AUTHOR NOTE

Alfie's story would never have been possible if the person who found her near death on his lawn had not called a wildlife rehabilitation organization. Such organizations save countless wild lives. I helped found a wildlife rescue and rehab group when I was in my twenties. It's still going strong.

Find out who to call in your community and keep their number handy so there's no time lost if you find a baby bird or other animal who needs help. (But first make sure they are really in distress and that no parents are nearby.)

Meanwhile, get to know the creatures who carry on their lives in your yard and near your home. Enjoy their beauty, respect their lives, and be kind to their presence.